NONPROFIT LEADERSHIP SUCCESS

A SHORT GUIDE TO BIG RESULTS

JEFF CONROY

NONPROFIT LEADERSHIP SUCCESS

A SHORT GUIDE TO BIG RESULTS

JEFF CONROY

An Honorée Corder Bespoke Book Production
Designed by Dino Marino, www.dinomarinodesign.com.

Paperback ISBN: 979-8-9908012-0-2
E-book ISBN: 979-8-9908012-2-6

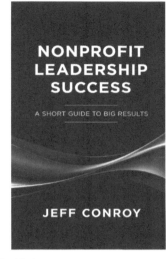

HOW TO USE THIS BOOKMARK:

1. Jot down ideas.

2. Note what you'd like to work on with your coach.

3. Capture action items that need your attention!

THANKS FOR READING!

Notes:

_____

_____

_____

_____

_____

_____

_____

_____

_____

_____

Notes:

_____

_____

_____

_____

_____

_____

_____

_____

_____

_____

_____

_____

_____

_____

_____

_____

_____

_____

CONROY LEADERSHIP
—— CONSULTING ——

To Jeannette

TABLE OF CONTENTS

SPECIAL INVITATION

Visit:
ConroyLeadershipConsulting.com/Discovery
to schedule a complimentary
laser coaching session.

INTRODUCTION

Let's cut to the chase. As a nonprofit leader, you don't have time for fluff.

You spend your days running meetings, dealing with staff members, preparing for (and recovering from) board meetings, setting budgets, communicating with staff, stakeholders, and clients, and a hundred other things.

You want to grow your organization and improve your leadership. But you don't want to waste time with coaches or consultants who don't have real-world experience.

As you already know, the nonprofit world is filled with advisers who are long on theory but short on experience.

Many have never run a nonprofit, been accountable to a board, led staff, developed a budget, or created a giving campaign. Yet, somehow, they feel equipped to tell *you* how to do it!

That's what sets me apart as a coach for nonprofits. For over three decades, I've led successfully in this area. For twenty of those years, I was a nonprofit CEO. I've been in leadership roles in just about every size of nonprofit, from small community organizations to large national ones.

Anyone who thinks they can advise a nonprofit without ever having run one is sorely mistaken. They can do much more damage than good.

I've been in your shoes. I know what the daily struggle is like. I also know what it's like to win big and stand alongside a team that has accomplished amazing things.

In the chapters ahead, I'll share some actionable tips and stories to improve your leadership. I'll also invite you on a journey to discover how to transform your leadership, and your nonprofit organization, through the power of coaching.

Let's get started!

CHAPTER ONE

YOUR BRIDGE TO NONPROFIT SUCCESS

In my work as a coach for nonprofits, I've gathered hundreds of stories over the years about how I've helped executives and leaders become more successful. Success is different for everyone; however, I'm sure we can agree it includes achieving an organization's goals while delivering on its mission while maintaining a manageable stress level, retaining staff, and avoiding burnout (among many other challenges).

Let me begin this chapter by sharing one success story that stands out.

I was engaged with a particular organization for nearly a year when the CEO reached out to me seeking assistance with their structure and organization. He was frustrated that his middle managers weren't effectively engaging with the frontline teams.

During my initial week with them, I observed a recurring pattern: the CEO would bypass middle management and directly issue instructions to the frontline staff, sidelining his leadership team.

When I pointed this out, he hadn't even realized he was doing it!

Over the ensuing months, I focused on coaching the CEO on proper delegation to his leadership team. I also worked with the leadership team on delegating effectively to the frontline workers, empowering them to excel in their roles. At the same time, I provided guidance to the frontline team on enhancing their teamwork and initiative-taking skills.

I introduced them to the concept of "extreme ownership," popularized by former US Navy

SEAL Jocko Willink in his book of the same name, *Extreme Ownership*. The concept can be summarized like this:

> Extreme ownership means taking full responsibility for everything within your purview. Successes are credited to the team, while failures are owned by the leader.

After nearly six months of embracing this new leadership philosophy, the nonprofit experienced a remarkable transformation. A newfound structure and greater accountability permeated the entire organization.

How did this team improve their leadership, communication, and delegation skills? How did they get from here to there?

It sounds simplistic, but it's not simple: I built a bridge for them and invited them to bravely walk across, trusting me, and that all would be better because of it.

EVERY LEADER NEEDS A BRIDGE

Since you're reading this book, you're probably already open to the idea of working with a coach. And I'm sure you already understand how coaching works and how it can help you.

That being said, I want to use this image of a *bridge* to visually illustrate how I help people—and specifically how I can help you.

Imagine you're standing on one side of a big chasm. You desperately want to get to the other side, but you're not sure how.

You don't have the tools, time, resources, or energy to build a bridge yourself. What do you do? You enlist the help of someone who knows bridges!

Imagine how relieved you'll feel when someone comes along with the material, know-how, and expertise to actually build the bridge you need to get to your destination.

Let me enhance the image just a bit. You're not standing on the edge of the chasm alone. Behind you, there are hundreds, perhaps thousands, of people waiting for you to figure out how you're going to take them across.

That's a great analogy for what it's like to lead a nonprofit. Those people behind you represent the staff, volunteers, board, stakeholders, constituents, and community members who are involved with your nonprofit.

If you can get a bridge built and lead them across, you can write a whole new future for your organization!

This book is the bridge between what you know and what you don't. I'm here to help fill in the gaps so you can start leading more effectively and enjoying the amazing results when you do so.

A BIT ABOUT ME

Let me share a few details about my background to set the context for who I am and how I can help you.

I attribute the Boy Scouts of America (BSA) for my foundational knowledge of nonprofits. Every executive at the BSA attends an annual weeklong training to learn about the administrative side of the organization in detail.

In the sixteen years I spent with the organization, I built a deeper knowledge about finances, endowments, recruiting, board development, and working with the media, to name just a few.

After the Boy Scouts, I was the executive director of the local United Way, where I learned through trial and error how to work with the community. I gained experience in building committees, putting on events, and raising millions of dollars.

In my work with St. Vincent's de Paul, I learned about obtaining federal grants and working within programs at the governmental and nongovernmental levels. All in all, I've worked with nonprofits at the federal, state, county, city, and neighborhood levels.

I attribute my emphasis on servant leadership to my master's degree in organizational leadership from Gonzaga University, in addition to some doctoral work.

You can have all the knowledge in the world, but at the end of the day you must be able to work with people. In my thirty-four years of nonprofit leadership and coaching, I've developed knowledge and mastery I'm happy to put to work on your behalf.

Let's turn our attention to a question that's probably been on your mind as you've been reading: Why work with a coach in the first place?

Keep reading to find out!

CHAPTER ONE TAKEAWAY

In your nonprofit leadership,
take "extreme ownership" for your personal
and organizational success.
It will transform your leadership
and inspire everyone around you.

CHAPTER ONE EXERCISE

1. Read *Extreme Ownership* by Jocko Willinck.

2. Identify three ways you can put the Extreme Ownership concept into practice.

CHAPTER TWO

UNLEASH YOUR POTENTIAL THROUGH COACHING

You're a nonprofit leader because you're confident and assertive. You want to make a difference in the world. You're ready and willing to deal with the unique challenges of nonprofits.

With the incredible skills and talent you already bring to the table, you might be wondering why you need a coach in the first place. Let me share three reasons why it's a great decision.

1. REAL-TIME CONVERSATIONS

Think back over the last week. Did you deal with any problems? Were there any situations you hadn't encountered before? Do you wish you could have talked to someone about them but didn't know where to turn?

That's the beauty of having a coach. You have someone on speed dial to come alongside you and help you process the day-to-day issues you're dealing with.

One of my current clients has been having issues with her staff and board. Many times on our calls, she has asked, "Do you have anything that can help me with this?"

In those moments, I'll share an insight, a resource, or some other tool I've come across to help them with the problem.

On a recent call, she shared a specific concern about an overbearing board member. She asked how she should deal with it.

I said, "First of all, board members have a lot of rights. Do you use *Robert's Rules of Order?*"

She replied, "No. I haven't heard of it."

I continued, "*Robert's Rules* is a guide for operating your board when it comes to rules and protocol. There's a process to all of this. If you need to dismiss a board member, there's a process for doing that as well. Robert's Rules help facilitate an effective outcome."[1]

I have these kinds of conversations all the time—real-time questions and answers providing immediate help. I invite my coaching clients to get in touch with me when they have questions or challenges so they can get help as soon as possible.

2. A GUARDRAIL FOR YOUR ORGANIZATION

It sounds harsh, but it's true: most nonprofit CEOs don't really know what they're doing.

I don't mean it as an insult but as a warning that your book knowledge and advanced degrees are not going to be enough to navigate all the sticky situations you'll encounter as a leader.

---

1. I recommend visiting https://robertsrules.com to view and purchase various editions of *Robert's Rules of Order*.

> When a new-to-you situation occurs,
> you won't want to wing it. No, "fake it
> till you make it" won't work either.
> You want to get it right the first time.

The truth is, there could be serious, irreversible, or even costly consequences if you handle a situation improperly. In nonprofit leadership, you definitely don't want to upset the wrong people, make a dire financial mistake, or deal ineffectively with a negative situation. It's easy to act out of pure emotion or make an amateur mistake without proper counsel.

I can't begin to count all the nonprofit leaders I've known over the years who made dumb mistakes that resulted in them losing a job and hurting the organization. I don't want that to happen to you.

3. RESOURCES TO IMPROVE YOUR LEADERSHIP

A local organization reached out to me for help with their executive team's time management. They were growing fast and struggling to keep up.

Each of its leaders had their own style, so I crafted a personalized time management plan for every one of them.

Some liked the Eisenhower Matrix, where they could prioritize tasks based on urgency and importance, and then switch things around as needed.

Others found the worksheets from Lee Cockerell's *Time Management Magic* helpful. They could jot down their daily goals and tasks, ticking them off as they went along. Anything left undone became the top priority for the next day.

For those who preferred simplicity, I offered a basic task management sheet. They just needed to list their daily tasks, set start and finish dates, and update the list each morning.

All of this sounds pretty straightforward. However, this team was so caught up in day-to-day tasks that they struggled to figure out simple systems to manage their time better.

Sometimes it takes an outside observer to give you a simple solution to a vexing problem.

Why work with a coach? Because you probably won't uncover these solutions on your own. Our tendency is to keep doing the same things over and over again while expecting different results.

Having an ally whose agenda is 100 percent your agent, someone who will provide unbiased feedback you can use to proactively achieve greater success and avoid or navigate frustrating challenges, will be worth their weight in gold.

Now that I've given the foundation for why you should consider hiring a coach, let's explore how to find the perfect one to partner with.

CHAPTER TWO TAKEAWAY

You aren't meant to go it alone,
and you don't need to figure out everything
yourself. Take advantage
of the resources, tools, and coaching available
to become more effective.

CHAPTER TWO EXERCISE

1. Learn more about *Robert's Rules of Order* and use them in your next meeting.

2. Jot down three situations where you would have benefited from having a coach.

CHAPTER THREE

THE PERFECT PARTNER FOR YOUR SUCCESS

The Walt Disney Co. is one of the most valuable entertainment brands in the world. With a vast network of theme parks, movies, merchandise, and the world's most valuable intellectual property, the company is a juggernaut of business.

And to think it all began with a mouse!

However, the mouse that's now the most recognized character in the world was not the sole, or even first, creation of Walt Disney.

In the late 1920s, Disney faced a critical setback that threatened to derail his burgeoning animation career. He had been working for

Universal Pictures on a series of live-action shorts when he and his lead animator, Ub Iwerks, developed a new character, Oswald Rabbit.

After the first Oswald cartoon was finished, Disney entered into a contract dispute with Universal because they wanted the character redesigned. Disney was removed from the series in 1928 and vowed to never again work on a character he could not own.

Soon afterward, Disney was on a train ride and sketched out the character he would later dub "Mickey Mouse." He gave the sketch to Iwerks, who created a more refined version, which made its historic first appearance in the animated short Steamboat Willie.

Without the talent and creative input from Ub Iwerks, one could argue that Mickey Mouse would have never made his film debut, and the Walt Disney Co. wouldn't be where it is today.

> When you find the perfect
> partner, adviser, or coach,
> it makes all the difference.

LEADERSHIP CAN BE LONELY

"It's lonely at the top" is an often-used phrase for a reason. Nonprofit leadership can be lonely. No one really understands what you go through on a daily basis.

It's not uncommon for me to consult with leaders and hear something like this: "Nobody understands what I do as a CEO. They might know my job description, but they don't realize what it takes to make it happen. I'm so glad I have someone to talk to about my situation."

One of my coaching clients recently remarked, "It's nice to actually talk to somebody who's been through it, who understands where I'm coming from. That's what sets you apart."

That's why I emphasize to nonprofit leaders that I understand what they're going through.

I have a good friend who is a nonprofit director. Some of his board members are unhappy with his leadership. They've been calling for his job. I told him, "I've been there! You have to surround yourself with *your people*."

I advised my friend to meet one-on-one with his board members to help mitigate the pack mentality. If you're in a board meeting and all twelve board members are starting to pounce on you, you need to work individually with them.

In my more than three decades in nonprofit leadership, I've experienced a lot. I can relate to just about anything you have been through in nonprofit leadership.

THE RAPPER AT THE COUNTY FAIR

One time, I received a call from a fair director in a conservative community. She had invited a famous rapper to perform, and this led to considerable anxiety among local residents.

She'd received numerous emails, phone calls, and even death threats in response to her decision. As a result, she was clearly upset and frustrated during our conversation.

I advised her, "It seems like it's just a vocal minority. I think you should stand your ground and engage with these church leaders individually."

She followed this advice, meeting with local church leaders and coordinating with law enforcement. Following the event, she reported that, according to police security, it was the most orderly event the fair had ever hosted.

> When you're in the middle of a crisis, you don't need a coach who has only read about problem-solving. You need somebody who has led from the trenches and can speak from experience.

At various times, I've been accused of things. My reputation has taken a hit. I've managed conflicts of every kind. But I've also led successful initiatives, planned high-profile events, and experienced great successes.

When I coach someone, I bring all of myself—the good experiences and the bad ones, too. I understand what it's like to walk in your shoes.

Do I have the titles and education? Sure. But more importantly, I have the heart and understanding to guide you even in the hardest of times.

That's what a true partnership looks like.

CHAPTER THREE TAKEAWAY

Just like Walt Disney needed to look no further
than his creative partner
Ub Iwerks to solve his problem,
you, too, have resources all around you
to help navigate tough situations.

CHAPTER THREE EXERCISE

1. Write down a list of your true partners. Consider how a coach could round out any open spots.

2. Review your list of board members and set up lunch or coffee meetings to connect with them at a deeper level.

CHAPTER FOUR

SEIZING THE MOMENT

One of the most successful movies of the 1990s was *Apollo 13*, which dramatized the doomed lunar mission that almost cost three astronauts their lives.

The crew of James "Jim" Lovell Jr., John "Jack" Swigert, and Fred Haise faced countless problems on their journey to return safely to Earth while packed into their crippled lunar module. The tiny vessel wasn't meant to hold three people for several days.

One of the final challenges they faced was entering back into Earth's orbit at just the right angle. If the angle was too steep, they would burn up in the atmosphere. If it was too shallow, they would bounce off the atmosphere like a skipping stone.

The only way to get it right was to depend on information from NASA's Mission Control to know how long, and at what time, to burn their engines. There was no way to figure it out on their own.

Timing was everything. If they didn't get it right, they were doomed. The whole world was watching, and the stakes couldn't have been any higher.

Fortunately, the Apollo 13 crew made it safely back to Earth and gave us a space exploration story for the ages!

You may not be stuck in a crippled spacecraft, but the stakes are still high for you.

> Every leader, and every nonprofit, faces
> critical moments when their success—
> or even their very survival—
> hangs in the balance.
> That's why good timing is critical.

Effective nonprofit leadership isn't just about navigating challenges. It is also about capitalizing on opportunities!

As we talk about working with a coach, it's important to recognize the moments when this decision can mean the difference between stagnation and growth. Let's look at four of them.

1. WHEN YOU'RE ON A GROWTH TRAJECTORY

Perhaps you have moved up to a larger nonprofit but have a similar role as before. Anytime you move into a role where you have a bigger staff, budget, facilities, and responsibilities, you also need a bigger mindset.

You'll also be dealing with a new board. Although there will certainly be similarities in processes and procedures from your previous experience, you'll benefit from coaching on how to develop and upgrade your board.

2. WHEN YOU'RE TRANSITIONING INTO A NEW ROLE

Maybe you've recently accepted a new leadership position in a nonprofit, or you're getting ready to. This is a fantastic time to use a coach so you set yourself up for success and avoid developing bad habits.

Even if you're not the CEO, but you're beginning a new role as an HR director, executive director, or head of development, you're heading into new territory.

> Always remember this simple truth:
> No matter your role, nonprofit leadership
> is *all about working with people.*
> And no two people are the same.

That's why this is a great time to have a series of conversations with a coach!

Note to CEOs: Hiring a coach for your top leaders can provide the same benefits for them as they can for you.

3. WHEN YOU NEED A TUNE-UP

Maybe you've been in your current role for a long time, but you can sense your passion and energy flagging. You feel unmoored and have lost your sense of purpose.

Or you might be dealing with a range of issues dragging the organization down. Management team issues, problems with staff development, vision misalignment with the board—these can all drain your energy and cause serious problems.

A great coach can help you work through issues and reenergize your leadership.

4. WHEN YOU'RE READY TO ACCEPT COACHING

You might have many years of experience in your nonprofit leadership role, but that doesn't mean you have it all figured out. One of the most important qualities of a good leader is the self-awareness to know they could benefit from a coach or adviser.

I've worked with my share of people who want a coach but don't want to listen to my advice. They tell me they want to change, they want to do better, but they don't want to listen to solid guidance.

When you're humble enough to accept coaching, that's a great time to engage a coach.

These are four critical moments when a coach could make a huge difference in your success.

But even when you feel things are going smoothly, there's always room for improvement. And as all nonprofit leaders know, there's a surprise around every corner. That's why it is important to seize the moment and engage with a coach who can help.

CHAPTER FOUR TAKEAWAY

Take a moment to reflect on where you've been and where you're going in your leadership journey. If you're at a natural transition point, how can you set yourself up for the greatest success?

CHAPTER FOUR EXERCISE

1. Identify where you are now versus where you want to go, and imagine how a coach could help you get there faster and easier.

2. What are your organization's three biggest opportunities right now? What are yours?

CHAPTER FIVE

INCREASING YOUR IMPACT

In the previous chapter, I talked about times when you might consider working with a coach. I mentioned one of those times is when you're poised for growth but aren't quite sure how to get there.

I recently collaborated with a local children's organization. Over two days, we dove into their plans for growth and dug into their current structure and job descriptions. We also hashed out ideas for their long-term vision.

During this process it became clear that their current organizational structure wasn't adequate if they wanted to expand. They faced a problem common to nonprofits: people were wearing too many hats, but there were not enough heads to go around.

As a result, I suggested bringing in an office manager to handle timecards, time off, and other HR needs. Meanwhile, we reorganized daily tasks among the team, with the manager overseeing all these details.

Here's the good news: with this new setup, the organization now has more room to grow and impact more lives than ever before! This is a perfect illustration of the key to increasing your organization's impact:

> If you want to grow, you need a trusted partner who helps you see the options.

Let's dive into the two elements of this statement.

A TRUSTED PARTNER

Every nonprofit leader has doubts, questions, and frustrations. Sometimes all at the same moment! When you need someone to talk to, who are you going to call?

Hint: not the Ghostbusters. It's also probably not your spouse, board members, executive team, staff members, volunteers, or donors. Although all those people play an important role in your life or in the organization, they can't play the role of an objective observer.

Instead, you need a trusted partner, an ally who is a confidant, a coach, and a safety valve all rolled into one.

That's why I tell my coaching clients to call, text, or email me anytime. I've had clients call me as they're walking into a meeting. "Hey, this meeting is about to start and we're going to address X, Y, and Z. I was going to handle it a certain way, but I'm not sure. What do you think?"

After we talk it through, they go into the meeting with more confidence because they have learned a better way to address things.

Another example: Small nonprofits are usually passion projects started by people with a heart who don't know how to raise money. They may not realize that most banks have a foundation that will donate $2,500 if they just fill out a grant application.

That's one tiny bit of knowledge that can help you move your nonprofit forward—and a great example of why a trusted partner is so valuable.

WHO HELPS YOU SEE THE OPTIONS

When you're facing a hard decision or you're not sure how to move forward, you need options. But it's hard to see these options if you have limited experience and you're dealing with dozens of pressing issues at the same time.

One of the greatest inventions in the modern world is the Maps app available on every smartphone. No matter which specific app you use, it lets you zoom out and see options for different routes as you travel. This is helpful if you're driving through an unfamiliar area or you hit traffic on the interstate.

> The Maps app gives you a bird's-eye view of your situation so you can see various routes that will get you where you're going faster. That's exactly what a great coach does.

Let's say you need to dismiss a difficult board member. You can't just walk in and fire them. What do you do instead?

First, I recommend meeting with your board president. Then go into an executive session where you express your concerns with the member. The board should approach the individual for a conversation.

In this example, you can see the value of not reacting out of emotion, but instead slowing down the process and being more intentional.

In the nonprofit world, emotions can run high because those who work or volunteer in an organization bring a deep passion for making a difference. Most nonprofits are passion projects at heart.

Working with a trusted adviser who helps you see the big picture and presents options can mean the difference between solving a big problem and making it worse.

Speaking of options, in the next chapter, I'll share a few of them on how we can work together to help you grow and begin increasing your impact.

CHAPTER FIVE TAKEAWAY

Think about a tough situation you're dealing
with right now. How helpful would it be to
have more options for solving
the problem or handling the issue?

CHAPTER FIVE EXERCISE

1. What are three situations you'd love the opportunity to talk through with a coach?

2. Take a moment to schedule a complimentary laser coaching session with me at ConroyLeadershipConsulting. com/Discovery to get a sense of what it's like to work with a coach.

CHAPTER SIX

CHARTING YOUR COURSE

We've covered a lot of ground in *Nonprofit Leadership Success*, and we're heading toward the home stretch. So far, you've learned:

- A bit about me and the value I bring to the table

- Why hiring a coach is the best way to transform your leadership and organization

- The tangible benefits you'll experience as a result of working together

- Practical takeaways that can improve your nonprofit immediately

In this chapter, I'll share three specific ways we can collaborate, depending on your needs and budget. You'll also learn how we can begin the process of working together.

INDIVIDUAL COACHING

This option gives you personalized, one-on-one help with whatever issues you're facing in your leadership and organization. We will meet at least thirty minutes per week. You also have the opportunity to call, text, or email me anytime you want.

For example, if you have a big meeting coming up, I'll invite you to call me right before for a pep talk or to walk through specific agenda items.

In addition, I'll give you a DiSC behavior assessment, which helps you understand your behavior and leadership in a deeper way.

Sometimes when I work with people, they ask if their executive staff can take the DiSC assessment also. The answer is YES! It costs extra, but the upside is that I can include the whole team on one report and teach you how to work and communicate better.

I recently did this with a hospital executive team of fifty people. They had a blast learning and growing together! It's a good reflection of how I view coaching:

> Coaching is a true partnership where we're working together to help identify where you most want to grow and practical ways to get there.

GROUP COACHING

Sometimes individual coaching is not in your budget. In that case, you might be a great candidate for my Nonprofit Leadership Circle, my group coaching program.

In this format, a group of nonprofit leaders attend weekly calls on critical issues for nonprofit leaders. I often bring guest experts to teach on specific topics, such as social media, time management, fundraising, working with your board, and many others.

With both individual and group coaching, my goal is to help you work through issues in real-time. We ask questions such as:

- How did last week go?
- What do you have coming up this week?
- What problems are you seeing right now?
- What hurdles or barriers are you dealing with?
- What tools or resources would be most helpful to you right now?

As a nonprofit leader, you're dealing with constant curve balls and unexpected challenges. Whether we work together individually or in a group setting, I'm here to help you become stronger and more effective.

12-WEEK PROGRAM

If you're looking for an option for your executive team or board, my 12-week program is exactly what you need. It features weekly meetings where we guide an individual or a small team through discussions on building culture and enhancing customer service.

Each week, we cover different topics, such as valuing your team, motivating your team, training and development, innovation, and shaping your leadership style, among others.

YOUR NEXT STEP

If you're ready to take the next step, I invite you to contact me. I respond very quickly to messages and would love to have a conversation about how I can help.

Whether we meet in person or set up a Zoom call, that initial conversation is vital to make sure you're in the right place to make the most of coaching. I also want to ensure we're a good fit.

I look forward to talking with you!

CHAPTER SIX TAKEAWAY

Wherever you are in your nonprofit
leadership journey, there are always pathways
and opportunities for growth.
I'm confident I can help you get there.

CHAPTER SIX EXERCISE

1. Consider which kind of coaching would be most helpful: individual, group, or a 12-week program.

2. How could you and your organization be different a year from now if you took advantage of focused coaching?

CHAPTER SEVEN

WHICH PATH WILL YOU CHOOSE?

In Robert Frost's famous poem *The Road Not Taken*, we meet an unnamed traveler standing at a crossroads. He writes:

> Two roads diverged in a yellow wood,
>
> And sorry I could not travel both
>
> And be one traveler, long I stood
>
> And looked down one as far as I could
>
> To where it bent in the undergrowth.

He considers the other road, knowing he must choose. For a moment, he tries to avoid the decision, vowing he'll come back later and travel the road he doesn't take today.

Then the traveler realizes the truth we all must accept in a moment of decision: We'll never return to this moment. So we must decide and take the next step.

Frost concludes the poem with these haunting words:

> I shall be telling this with a sigh
>
> Somewhere ages and ages hence:
>
> Two roads diverged in a wood, and I—
>
> I took the one less traveled by,
>
> And that has made all the difference.

Just like the traveler in the woods, you also stand at a crossroads. Before you, there are two paths.

Most nonprofit leaders choose the *well-traveled road*. It's the path of struggle where they try to figure everything out themselves.

This journey ends in frustration because they keep doing the same things over and over but expect different results. It rarely works.

I challenge you to take *the road less traveled*. Successful nonprofit leaders take this path because they don't have to travel it alone. They understand the value of having a great coach walk alongside them.

They will also arrive at their destination much faster because they've had access to more guidance, tools, and wisdom than ever before. Best of all, they feel more excited about their mission to change lives.

Look at your calendar one year from today. Where do you want to be in your leadership? Where do you want your organization to be?

That date will come and go, but will you and your organization look much different than they do today?

I would be honored to come alongside you as you travel the road to more vitality, transformation, and growth. I encourage you to get in touch.

GRATITUDE

To Jeannette, for the years of patience, love, and support. You are the CEO of Conroy Leadership Consulting. I'm just the "talent." To the moon and back! #TeamConroy

To Monica, Brianne, and John, thank you for listening to my leadership quotes, theories, and ideas growing up and saying, "You need to write a book, but work on your spelling." I love you guys!

To Erik and Paul, welcome to the family. The man who is fortunate in his choice of son-in-law gains a son. Love you both.

To my grandkids, Evelyn and Leif, I hope you read this when you're older. Leaders read. It's good for the brain, and good for the soul.

And finally, to Honorée, Kent, M.J., Mike, and Jen, thank you for helping bring my book to life!

WOULD YOU REVIEW THIS BOOK?

If you enjoyed reading *Nonprofit Leadership Success*, would you kindly take a few moments to leave a review wherever you purchased it (and perhaps even Goodreads.com)? I'm grateful for your support. Thank you!

WHO IS JEFF CONROY?

With a 30-plus-year background in the nonprofit sector, holding executive roles at the Boy Scouts of America, United Way of Kootenai County, and St. Vincent de Paul North Idaho, Jeff has now shifted his focus to aiding various organizations.

He delivers value by sharing his expertise and emphasizing the importance of small, impactful actions. As a coach, presenter, and facilitator, Jeff is committed to two key principles: fostering leadership through coaching and mentoring, and establishing robust, long-lasting partnerships with those he works with.

These connections are more than just professional courtesies. They are the ties that foster excellence.

Jeff lives in Dalton Gardens, Idaho. He and his wife, Jeannette, love spending time with family, including his two grandkids, Evelyn and Leif. Jeff loves reading about great leadership and all things Disney. He is also a member of the long-standing No More Leadership BS Podcast team.

Website: https://conroyleadershipconsulting.com
Email: jeff@conroyleadershipconsulting.com
Phone: (208) 215-6285

I'd love to discuss how we can work together.

HIRE JEFF

With over 30 years of nonprofit experience, from frontline roles to spearheading state-wide projects, Jeff is the coach you need to enhance your leadership skills. Ready to begin?

Visit <u>ConroyLeadershipConsulting.com</u>

to get started.

Made in United States
Troutdale, OR
08/02/2024